AR=5.1    PTS=.5    Quiz=104330

# Born to be Wild
# Little Donkeys

Ariane Chottin

Words that appear in the glossary are printed in
**boldface** type the first time they occur in the text.

PUBLISHING
A Member of the WRC Media Family of Companies

# A Big Family

Donkeys belong to the same animal family as horses, ponies, and zebras. They look a lot like small horses. Some donkeys are big and stand 5 feet (152 centimeters) tall. Others are very short, measuring only about 31 inches (79 cm) tall — the size of a large dog. The most common donkey is between 3 and 4 feet (90 and 120 cm) tall. Donkeys have thin legs, a dip in their backs, and a rounded belly. They have small but strong hooves. Donkeys can be many colors, depending on their **breed**. Some are gray, others are brown, beige, black, or have small marks or spots on their coats. Although most donkeys have short, straight hair, some are covered with long, curly hair.

**Donkeys look like horses, but, compared to the size of their bodies, donkeys have bigger heads and much longer ears than horses.**

## What do you think?

Why are donkeys so small?

a) because they do not grow big

b) because they do not eat much food

c) because they have a hard life

3

## Donkeys are small because they have a hard life.

Donkeys may be small, but they are very sturdy animals. Animals that are small and strong seem to be better at living and surviving in difficult places. Today, most donkeys are **domesticated**, but some donkeys in Asia and Africa still live in the wild. Some live in rocky mountains. Others live in stony deserts, where the weather can be hot, very little rain falls, and only a few plants grow. Donkeys are herbivores, which means they eat only plants.

**An onager is a type of wild donkey. Onagers live in the mountains of some Asian countries.**

A poitou (PWA-too) donkey lives in western France. It is the largest kind of donkey. The poitou's long, thick fur protects it from cold weather and rain. A baby poitou looks like a stuffed toy animal.

The donkeys in China and other parts of Asia have light-colored coats and dark manes that grow thicker in winter.

Wild donkeys from Africa are the **ancestors** of all of today's donkey breeds. Donkeys were domesticated by humans about six thousand years ago.

5

# A Mom Called Jenny

A female donkey is called a jennet or a jenny. Jennies that become mothers carry their babies inside their bodies for one year. When a jenny is ready to give birth, she moves away from the other donkeys she lives with. After her baby, or foal, is born, the jenny takes very good care of it. She licks the foal right after it is born to clean its wet coat and to help it stand up. The little foal is unsteady at first, but it can stand up just thirty minutes after it is born. When it needs to rest, it snuggles against its mother's side.

## What do you think?

Who does a newborn foal live with?

a) its mother and father

b) its cousins

c) its parents and a herd, or group, of other family members

A jenny usually gives birth to only one foal each year, but, in rare cases, a jenny may have two babies at the same time.

**A newborn foal lives with its parents and a herd of other family members.**

A herd of donkeys is made up of about fifteen jennies, several foals, and the male, called a jack, that is the father of all the foals. Sometimes, other males live with the family, but the **dominant** male watches over the herd and decides when the herd must move. Donkey foals are lively and playful. Since most foals in the herd are born at about the same time, they all play together. The foals are also naturally affectionate and seem to show what they are feeling.

Like its mother, a little donkey is cautious and fearful. It never strays too far from its family, and when anything disturbs the foal, it jumps.

When a donkey herd arrives at a pasture, the donkeys spread out so each animal can **graze** by itself. When they need to find water, however, the leader of the herd gathers the donkeys together, and they all follow him.

A donkey foal becomes an adult after about two years. It will then leave its mother and its family herd and join a new herd, so it can start its own family.

9

# A Prickly Menu

In the high places and hot regions where many donkeys live, grass is often dry and hard to find. Donkeys can, however, find all kinds of thorny plants to eat, including thistles and many kinds of **prickly** shrubs. These plants are full of moist, vitamin-rich sap. A little donkey learns from its mother which plants are best to eat. When it eats a plant, a donkey gently curls its lips so the plant's thorns won't hurt them. Then it pushes its teeth forward to bite off the plant. The donkey chews the plant long enough to get all the juicy sap out of it.

Donkeys have very long **intestines**, which help them **digest** plants slowly, absorbing as many **nutrients** as possible.

## What do you think?

**Why do donkeys eat thistles?**

a) because thistles are full of thorns

b) because thistles help keep them healthy

c) because thistles clean donkeys' teeth

Donkeys eat thistles because thistles help keep them healthy.

Foals get the nutrients they need from their mothers' rich milk. They drink as much as they want for about one year. Although foals do not eat a lot of other foods, they are curious about them. Little donkeys like the taste of grass, but they also need to learn what to eat when grass cannot be found. During the first year, jennies stay with their foals and teach them to recognize the other kinds of plants they can eat.

To live through **droughts**, donkeys drink water whenever they can. Like camels, they are able to take in a lot of water at one time, then go many days without drinking again.

Little donkeys learn to eat many different foods.  Besides thistles, they eat grass, fruits, and vegetables, such as carrots.

This foal still has its baby teeth. Adult donkeys have thirty-six to forty-two teeth, and male donkeys have more teeth than females have.

13

# Tough Little Feet

At the ends of their long thin legs, donkey foals have tiny brown hooves. Their little hooves might look fragile, but they are strong enough for walking in the mountains. Thanks to their tough hooves, foals can walk far at a young age, and they are as tireless as their parents. Little donkeys follow their mothers on steep mountain slopes and along narrow trails. Donkeys move slowly, but surely. They rarely **gallop**, but they are able to walk for a very long time.

## What do you think?

Why are donkeys so good at walking on mountain paths?

a) because they are not afraid of heights

b) because they are small

c) because they have excellent memories

The tissues that surround the bones and muscles in a foal's legs are very flexible, which helps the foal stand for a long time without becoming tired. Sometimes, foals even sleep standing up.

## Donkeys are good at walking on mountain paths because they have excellent memories.

When donkeys walk through the mountains, they use their excellent memories to travel safely on difficult paths. They can remember every **obstacle** on a path perfectly and can decide which dangers they must avoid. When donkeys travel together as a herd, they walk single file. They can place their hooves in the middle of loose rocks without sliding, and they never make a mistake because they take their time and know which way to go.

**Donkeys have amazing memories. They will never do anything a second time that they did not like the first time.**

Donkeys usually walk, but they sometimes jog, or even gallop, when they are frightened. When they run, donkeys can reach speeds of up to 40 miles (65 kilometers) an hour.

A donkey's hoof is a hard, thick toenail surrounding a single toe. The hoof, which is made of three layers of hard skin, is tough, elastic, and very stable.

17

# A Stylish Coat

A young donkey grows up quickly. Little by little, a coat of short, rough hair replaces its silky soft, fuzzy hair, but underneath its new coat, the donkey still has soft, light-colored hair. A donkey's brown-gray color blends well with its surroundings. Its coat is lighter on the stomach and the insides of its legs. Around the donkey's dark eyes are two circles of white hair. The tip of its nose is also covered with white hair. Donkeys have short, thick manes that stand straight up on the backs of their heads and necks.

**The end of a donkey's tail has thick, bushy hair. Donkeys use their tails to swat away flies and other insects that buzz around them.**

**What do you think?**

Why are a donkey's ears so big?

a) to detect dangers better

b) to make the donkey easier to see from a distance

c) to make the donkey's head look cute

Thanks to their outstanding hearing, donkeys are able to escape terrible dangers. They can easily hear large **predators**, such as wolves, lions, leopards, and tigers. Leopards watch for donkeys and wait near bodies of water to attack them. When their enemies come too close, donkeys stand on their hind legs and defend themselves with their front hooves. A kick from a donkey's hard hooves can cause an enemy severe wounds.

Donkeys have very good eyesight. With their eyes on the sides of their heads, donkeys can see all four of their feet at one time.

Donkeys can move their extra-large ears in different directions to detect the tiniest noises, even from a long distance away.

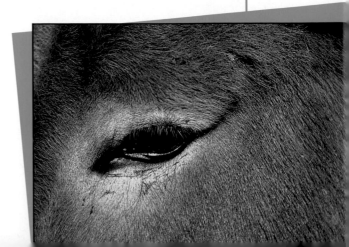

20

A donkey brays to warn other members of its herd of danger. Its bray —
*aw-EE*, *aw-EE* — is so loud that it can be heard from far away. Some people
use donkeys to guard herds of sheep, cattle, or goats. A donkey will bray
and chase and kick predators that come too close.

Donkeys are **mammals**. Domesticated donkeys live in all parts of the world, but most wild donkeys live in countries that have hot weather. Donkeys in the southwestern United States and Mexico are called by their Spanish name "burro." Wild donkeys are rare. Two kinds of wild donkeys can be found in the mountains of Central Asia, where they live at heights up to 20,000 feet (6,000 meters). One kind of wild donkey still lives in the deserts of Africa. Because there are only a few hundred of these animals, they are protected by law and cannot be hunted. In the wild, donkeys live twenty-five to thirty years. In captivity, they live forty to fifty years.

Donkeys are related to horses, ponies, and zebras.

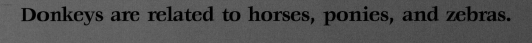

Donkeys have large ears that are sensitive to any noise.

A donkey's mane has short, stiff hair.

Donkeys' dark eyes are usually circled with white hair.

The weight of a donkey varies according to its breed and size, ranging from 330 to 990 pounds (150 to 450 kilograms).

At their shoulders, donkeys can be 30 to 60 inches (75 to 150 cm) tall.

A donkey has a long, thin tail that is bushy at the end.

Some donkeys have stripes on their legs. Most donkeys have dark lines around their ears and dark stripes on their backs and shoulders.

# GLOSSARY

**ancestors** — groups of animals in the past from which other, more current, groups come

**breed** — (n) a particular group of animals that all have the same physical features and abilities

**digest** — to break down food into a form that can be absorbed and used by the body

**domesticated** — tamed, not wild

**dominant** — having the most power or control

**droughts** — periods of little or no rain

**gallop** — to run on four legs at a fast speed

**graze** — to feed on growing grass and other plants

**intestines** — the parts of bodies where food is digested

**mammals** — warm-blooded animals that have backbones, give birth to live babies, feed their young milk from the mother's body, and have skin that is covered with hair or fur

**nutrients** — the parts of foods that help people and other animals grow and develop

**obstacle** — an object that blocks forward movement or makes movement difficult in some way

**predators** — animals that hunt and kill other animals for food

**prickly** — having sharp parts, such as thorns

Please visit our web site at: **www.garethstevens.com**
**For a free color catalog describing Gareth Stevens Publishing's list of high-quality books and multimedia programs, call 1-800-542-2595 (USA) or 1-800-387-3178 (Canada). Gareth Stevens Publishing's fax: (414) 332-3567.**

**Library of Congress Cataloging-in-Publication Data**

Chottin, Ariane.
    [Petit âne. English]
    Little donkeys / Ariane Chottin. — North American ed.
      p. cm. — (Born to be wild)
    ISBN 0-8368-6165-5 (lib. bdg.)
    1. Donkeys—Juvenile literature. 2. Foals—Juvenile literature.
    I. Title. II. Series.
    QL737.U6C4613   2006
    599.665—dc22              2005053152

This North American edition first published in 2006 by
**Gareth Stevens Publishing**
A Member of the WRC Media Family of Companies
330 West Olive Street, Suite 100
Milwaukee, Wisconsin 53212 USA

This U.S. edition copyright © 2006 by Gareth Stevens, Inc.
Original edition copyright © 2002 by Mango Jeunesse.

First published in 2002 as *Le petit âne* by Mango Jeunesse, an imprint of Editions Mango, Paris, France. Additional end matter copyright © 2006 by Gareth Stevens, Inc.

Picture Credits (t=top, b=bottom, l=left, r=right)
Bios: Klein/Hubert cover, title page, pages 2, 7, 15, 18, 22, back cover; Dani/Jeske 5(bl); Bergerot/Robert 5(br). Colibri: J. Delpech 9(b); P. Polette 13(both), 16, 20(l). Hoa-Qui: Zéfa 10. Jacana: J. Dragesco 4, 20(br); S. Cordier 5(t); A. Carrara 12; J. P. Thomas 22–23. Phone: Y. Lanceau 17(t); Fr. Nevoit 17(b), 21. Sunset: Animals Animals: G. Lacz 8; A. Christof 9(t).

English translation: Muriel Castille
Gareth Stevens editor: Barbara Kiely Miller
Gareth Stevens art direction: Tammy West
Gareth Stevens designer: Jenni Gaylord

Printed in the United States of America

1 2 3 4 5 6 7 8 9 10 09 08 07 06